THIS BOOK BELONGS TO

_____
NAME

_____
DATE

"YOU ARE FEARFULLY AND WONDERFULLY MADE"
PSALM 139:14

1 CHRONICLES 16:11

Look to the LORD
and his strength;
seek his face always.

DATE: _____

TODAY I AM GRATEFUL FOR:

TODAY'S SCRIPTURE READING

SCRIPTURE REFLECTIONS:

DEAR GOD,

I AM PRAYING FOR:

THIS IS THE CONFIDENCE WE HAVE IN APPROACHING GOD: THAT IF WE ASK ANYTHING ACCORDING TO HIS WILL,
HE HEARS US.

1 JOHN 5:14

DATE: _____

I HAVE SEEN THE HANDS OF GOD IN MY LIFE:

_____
_____
_____
_____
_____
_____

TODAY'S SCRIPTURE READING

SCRIPTURE REFLECTIONS:

PRAYER LIST:

_____
_____
_____
_____
_____

DEAR GOD,

Pray in the Spirit on all occasions with all kinds of prayers and requests. With this in mind, be alert and always keep on praying for all the Lord's people.

EPHESIANS 6:18

DATE: _____

I AM GRATEFUL FOR:

TODAY'S SCRIPTURE READING

_____

_____

SCRIPTURE REFLECTIONS:

_____

_____

_____

_____

DEAR GOD,

I AM PRAYING FOR

PERSONAL OTHERS

THEN YOU WILL CALL ON ME AND COME AND PRAY TO ME, AND I WILL LISTEN TO YOU.

JEREMIAH 29:12

DATE: _____

I HAVE SEEN THE HANDS OF GOD IN MY LIFE:

TODAY'S SCRIPTURE READING

_____
_____

SCRIPTURE REFLECTIONS:

_____
_____
_____
_____

DOODLE HOW YOU REALLY FEEL TODAY

AREAS YOU WANT TO WORK ON:

_____
_____
_____
_____

PSALM 9:9-10

The LORD is a refuge for the oppressed, a stronghold in times of trouble. Those who know your name trust in you, for you, LORD, have never forsaken those who seek you.

DATE: _____

TODAY I AM GRATEFUL FOR:

_____

_____

_____

_____

_____

_____

TODAY'S SCRIPTURE READING

SCRIPTURE REFLECTIONS:

DEAR GOD,

I AM PRAYING FOR:

_____

_____

_____

_____

_____

YOU WILL PRAY TO HIM,
AND HE WILL HEAR YOU,
AND YOU WILL FULFILL YOUR VOWS.

JOB 22:27

DATE: _____

I HAVE SEEN THE HANDS OF GOD IN MY LIFE:

_____
_____
_____
_____
_____
_____

TODAY'S SCRIPTURE READING

SCRIPTURE REFLECTIONS:

PRAYER LIST:

_____
_____
_____
_____
_____

DEAR GOD,

Is anyone among you in trouble? Let them pray. Is anyone happy? Let them sing songs of praise.

JAMES 5:13

DATE: _____

I AM GRATEFUL FOR: TODAY'S SCRIPTURE READING

_____
_____   SCRIPTURE REFLECTIONS:
_____
_____
_____
_____

DEAR GOD,

I AM PRAYING FOR
PERSONAL   OTHERS

> BUT I TELL YOU, LOVE YOUR ENEMIES AND PRAY FOR THOSE WHO PERSECUTE YOU.
>
> **MATTHEW 5:44**

DATE: _____

I HAVE SEEN THE HANDS OF GOD IN MY LIFE:

_____
_____
_____
_____
_____
_____

TODAY'S SCRIPTURE READING

SCRIPTURE REFLECTIONS:

DOODLE HOW YOU REALLY FEEL TODAY

AREAS YOU WANT TO WORK ON:

_____
_____
_____
_____

PROVERBS 15:8

The LORD detests the sacrifice of the wicked, but the prayer of the upright pleases him.

DATE: _____

TODAY I AM GRATEFUL FOR:

_____

_____

_____

_____

_____

TODAY'S SCRIPTURE READING

SCRIPTURE REFLECTIONS:

DEAR GOD,

I AM PRAYING FOR:

_____

_____

_____

_____

_____

MAY MY PRAYER BE
SET BEFORE YOU LIKE
INCENSE;
MAY THE LIFTING UP
OF MY HANDS BE
LIKE THE EVENING
SACRIFICE.

PSALM 141:2

DATE: _____

I HAVE SEEN THE HANDS OF GOD IN MY LIFE:

_____
_____
_____
_____
_____
_____

TODAY'S SCRIPTURE READING

SCRIPTURE REFLECTIONS:

PRAYER LIST:

_____
_____
_____
_____
_____

DEAR GOD,

One of those days Jesus went out to a mountainside to pray, and spent the night praying to God.

LUKE 6:12

DATE: _____

I AM GRATEFUL FOR:

TODAY'S SCRIPTURE READING

_____

_____

SCRIPTURE REFLECTIONS:

_____

_____

_____

_____

DEAR GOD,

I AM PRAYING FOR

PERSONAL   OTHERS

> ANSWER ME WHEN
> I CALL TO YOU,
> MY RIGHTEOUS GOD.
> GIVE ME RELIEF FROM
> MY DISTRESS;
> HAVE MERCY ON ME
> AND HEAR MY
> PRAYER.
>
> **PSALM 4:1**

DATE: _____

I HAVE SEEN THE HANDS OF GOD IN MY LIFE:

_____
_____
_____
_____
_____
_____

TODAY'S SCRIPTURE READING

SCRIPTURE REFLECTIONS:

DOODLE HOW YOU REALLY FEEL TODAY

AREAS YOU WANT TO WORK ON:

_____
_____
_____
_____

ROMANS 8:26

In the same way, the Spirit helps us in our weakness. We do not know what we ought to pray for, but the Spirit himself intercedes for us through wordless groans.

DATE: _____

TODAY I AM GRATEFUL FOR:

TODAY'S SCRIPTURE READING

_____

_____

SCRIPTURE REFLECTIONS:

_____

_____

_____

_____

DEAR GOD,

I AM PRAYING FOR:

_____

_____

_____

_____

_____

> DO NOT BE ANXIOUS ABOUT ANYTHING, BUT IN EVERY SITUATION, BY PRAYER AND PETITION, WITH THANKSGIVING, PRESENT YOUR REQUESTS TO GOD.
>
> PHILIPPIANS 4:6

DATE: _____

I HAVE SEEN THE HANDS OF GOD IN MY LIFE:

_____
_____
_____
_____
_____
_____

TODAY'S SCRIPTURE READING

SCRIPTURE REFLECTIONS:

PRAYER LIST:

_____
_____
_____
_____
_____

DEAR GOD,

Devote yourselves to prayer, being watchful and thankful.

COLOSSIANS 4:2

DATE: _____

I AM GRATEFUL FOR:

TODAY'S SCRIPTURE READING

_____

_____

SCRIPTURE REFLECTIONS:

_____

_____

_____

_____

DEAR GOD,

I AM PRAYING FOR

PERSONAL   OTHERS

> **THEREFORE, I WANT THE MEN EVERYWHERE TO PRAY, LIFTING UP HOLY HANDS WITHOUT ANGER OR DISPUTING.**
>
> I TIMOTHY 2:8

DATE: _____

I HAVE SEEN THE HANDS OF GOD IN MY LIFE:

_____
_____
_____
_____
_____
_____

TODAY'S SCRIPTURE READING

SCRIPTURE REFLECTIONS:

DOODLE HOW YOU REALLY FEEL TODAY

AREAS YOU WANT TO WORK ON:

_____
_____
_____
_____

JAMES 5:16

Therefore confess your sins to each other and pray for each other so that you may be healed. The prayer of a righteous person is powerful and effective.

DATE: _____

TODAY I AM GRATEFUL FOR:

TODAY'S SCRIPTURE READING

SCRIPTURE REFLECTIONS:

DEAR GOD,

I AM PRAYING FOR:

THIS IS THE CONFIDENCE WE HAVE IN APPROACHING GOD: THAT IF WE ASK ANYTHING ACCORDING TO HIS WILL, HE HEARS US.

1 JOHN 5:14

DATE: _____

I HAVE SEEN THE HANDS OF GOD IN MY LIFE:

_____
_____
_____
_____
_____
_____

TODAY'S SCRIPTURE READING

SCRIPTURE REFLECTIONS:

PRAYER LIST:

_____
_____
_____
_____
_____

DEAR GOD,

What then shall we say
to these things?
If God is for us,
who can be against us?

ROMANS 8:31

DATE: _____

I AM GRATEFUL FOR: TODAY'S SCRIPTURE READING

_____

_____   SCRIPTURE REFLECTIONS:

_____

_____

_____

_____

DEAR GOD,

I AM PRAYING FOR
PERSONAL   OTHERS

All Scripture is God-breathed and is useful for teaching, rebuking, correcting and training in righteousness, so that the servant of God may be thoroughly equipped for every good work.

2 Timothy 3:16-17

DATE: _____

I HAVE SEEN THE HANDS OF GOD IN MY LIFE:

_____
_____
_____
_____
_____
_____

TODAY'S SCRIPTURE READING

SCRIPTURE REFLECTIONS:

DOODLE HOW YOU REALLY FEEL TODAY

AREAS YOU WANT TO WORK ON:

_____
_____
_____
_____

ROMANS 12:12

Rejoice in hope, be patient in tribulation, be constant in prayer.

DATE: _____

TODAY I AM GRATEFUL FOR:

TODAY'S SCRIPTURE READING

_____

_____

SCRIPTURE REFLECTIONS:

_____

_____

_____

_____

DEAR GOD,

I AM PRAYING FOR:

_____

_____

_____

_____

_____

THE LORD IS MY STRENGTH AND MY SHIELD; MY HEART ATRUSTED IN HIM, AND I AM HELPED: THEREFORE, MY HEART GREATLY REJOICETH; AND WITH MY SONG WILL I PRAISE HIM.

PSALMS 28:7

DATE: _____

I HAVE SEEN THE HANDS OF GOD
IN MY LIFE:

TODAY'S SCRIPTURE READING

_____

_____   **SCRIPTURE REFLECTIONS:**

_____

_____

_____

PRAYER LIST:

_____

_____

_____

_____

_____

DEAR GOD,

Be strong and courageous. Do not be afraid or terrified, for the LORD your God goes with you; He will never leave you nor forsake you.

DEUTERONOMY 31:6

DATE: _____

I AM GRATEFUL FOR:

TODAY'S SCRIPTURE READING

_____

_____

SCRIPTURE REFLECTIONS:

_____

_____

_____

_____

DEAR GOD,

I AM PRAYING FOR

PERSONAL   OTHERS

"AH, SOVEREIGN LORD, YOU HAVE MADE THE HEAVENS AND THE EARTH BY YOUR GREAT POWER AND OUTSTRETCHED ARM. NOTHING IS TOO HARD FOR YOU."

JEREMIAH 29:12

DATE: _____

I HAVE SEEN THE HANDS OF GOD IN MY LIFE:

_____
_____
_____
_____
_____
_____

TODAY'S SCRIPTURE READING

SCRIPTURE REFLECTIONS:

DOODLE HOW YOU REALLY FEEL TODAY

AREAS YOU WANT TO WORK ON:

_____
_____
_____
_____

DEUTERONOMY 20:4

For the LORD your God is the one who goes with you to fight for you against your enemies to give you Victory.

DATE: _____

TODAY I AM GRATEFUL FOR: TODAY'S SCRIPTURE READING

_____

_____   SCRIPTURE REFLECTIONS:

_____

_____

_____

_____

DEAR GOD,

I AM PRAYING FOR:

_____

_____

_____

_____

_____

AND OUR HOPE FOR YOU IS FIRM, BECAUSE WE KNOW THAT JUST AS YOU SHARE IN OUR SUFFERINGS, SO ALSO YOU SHARE IN OUR COMFORT.

2 CORINTHIANS 1:7

DATE: _____

I HAVE SEEN THE HANDS OF GOD IN MY LIFE:

_____
_____
_____
_____
_____
_____

TODAY'S SCRIPTURE READING

SCRIPTURE REFLECTIONS:

PRAYER LIST:

_____
_____
_____
_____
_____

DEAR GOD,

My flesh and my heart
may fail,
but God is the strength
of my heart and
my portion forever.

PSALM 73:26

DATE: _____

I AM GRATEFUL FOR:

TODAY'S SCRIPTURE READING

_____

_____

SCRIPTURE REFLECTIONS:

_____

_____

_____

_____

DEAR GOD,

I AM PRAYING FOR

PERSONAL   OTHERS

> BUT THOSE WHO HOPE IN THE LORD WILL RENEW THEIR STRENGTH. THEY WILL SOAR ON WINGS LIKE EAGLES; THEY WILL RUN AND NOT GROW WEARY, THEY WILL WALK AND NOT BE FAINT.
>
> ISAIAH 40:31

DATE: _____

I HAVE SEEN THE HANDS OF GOD IN MY LIFE:

_____
_____
_____
_____
_____
_____

TODAY'S SCRIPTURE READING

SCRIPTURE REFLECTIONS:

DOODLE HOW YOU REALLY FEEL TODAY

AREAS YOU WANT TO WORK ON:

_____
_____
_____
_____

PSALM 46:1

God is our refuge and strength, an ever-present help in trouble.

DATE: _____

TODAY I AM GRATEFUL FOR:

TODAY'S SCRIPTURE READING

SCRIPTURE REFLECTIONS:

DEAR GOD,

I AM PRAYING FOR:

"MY GRACE IS SUFFICIENT FOR YOU, FOR MY POWER IS MADE PERFECT IN WEAKNESS." THEREFORE I WILL BOAST ALL THE MORE GLADLY ABOUT MY WEAKNESSES, SO THAT CHRIST'S POWER MAY REST ON ME. THAT IS WHY, FOR CHRIST'S SAKE, I DELIGHT IN WEAKNESSES, IN INSULTS, IN HARDSHIPS, IN PERSECUTIONS, IN DIFFICULTIES. FOR WHEN I AM WEAK, THEN I AM STRONG.

2 CORINTHIANS 12:9-10

DATE: _____

I HAVE SEEN THE HANDS OF GOD IN MY LIFE:

_____
_____
_____
_____
_____
_____

TODAY'S SCRIPTURE READING

SCRIPTURE REFLECTIONS:

PRAYER LIST:

_____
_____
_____
_____
_____

DEAR GOD,

Cast all your anxiety
on Him
because he cares
for you.

1 PETER 5:7

DATE: _____

I AM GRATEFUL FOR:

_____
_____
_____
_____
_____
_____

TODAY'S SCRIPTURE READING

SCRIPTURE REFLECTIONS:

DEAR GOD,

I AM PRAYING FOR

PERSONAL   OTHERS

> WHEN YOU PASS THROUGH THE WATERS,
> I WILL BE WITH YOU;
> AND WHEN YOU PASS THROUGH THE RIVERS, THEY WILL NOT SWEEP OVER YOU. WHEN YOU WALK THROUGH THE FIRE, YOU WILL NOT BE BURNED; THE FLAMES WILL NOT SET YOU ABLAZE.
>
> ISAIAH 43:2

DATE: _____

I HAVE SEEN THE HANDS OF GOD IN MY LIFE:

_____
_____
_____
_____
_____

TODAY'S SCRIPTURE READING

SCRIPTURE REFLECTIONS:

DOODLE HOW YOU REALLY FEEL TODAY

AREAS YOU WANT TO WORK ON:

_____
_____
_____
_____

MATTHEW 11:28

*Come to me,
all you who are weary
and burdened,
and I will give you rest.*

DATE: _____

TODAY I AM GRATEFUL FOR: TODAY'S SCRIPTURE READING

_____

_____   SCRIPTURE REFLECTIONS:

_____

_____

_____

_____

DEAR GOD,

I AM PRAYING FOR:

_____

_____

_____

_____

_____

**THE NAME OF THE LORD IS A FORTIFIED TOWER;
THE RIGHTEOUS RUN TO IT AND ARE SAFE.**

PROVERBS 18:10

DATE: _____

I HAVE SEEN THE HANDS OF GOD
IN MY LIFE:

TODAY'S SCRIPTURE READING

_____

_____

SCRIPTURE REFLECTIONS:

_____

_____

_____

_____

PRAYER LIST:

_____

_____

_____

_____

_____

DEAR GOD,

Truly I tell you,
if you have faith as small as
a mustard seed,
you can say to this mountain,
'Move from here to there,'
and it will move.
Nothing will be impossible
for you.

MATTHEW 17:20

DATE: _____

I AM GRATEFUL FOR: TODAY'S SCRIPTURE READING

_____

_____   SCRIPTURE REFLECTIONS:

_____

_____

_____

DEAR GOD,

I AM PRAYING FOR
PERSONAL   OTHERS

GREATER LOVE HAS NO ONE THAN THIS: TO LAY DOWN ONE'S LIFE FOR ONE'S FRIENDS.

JOHN 15:13

DATE: _____

I HAVE SEEN THE HANDS OF GOD IN MY LIFE:

_____
_____
_____
_____
_____
_____

TODAY'S SCRIPTURE READING

SCRIPTURE REFLECTIONS:

DOODLE HOW YOU REALLY FEEL TODAY

AREAS YOU WANT TO WORK ON:

_____
_____
_____
_____

2 CORINTHIANS 4:18

So we fix our eyes not on what is seen, but on what is unseen, since what is seen is temporary, but what is unseen is eternal.

DATE: _____

TODAY I AM GRATEFUL FOR:

TODAY'S SCRIPTURE READING

_____

_____

SCRIPTURE REFLECTIONS:

_____

_____

_____

DEAR GOD,

I AM PRAYING FOR:

_____

_____

_____

_____

_____

THEREFORE, MY DEAR BROTHERS AND SISTERS, STAND FIRM. LET NOTHING MOVE YOU. ALWAYS GIVE YOURSELVES FULLY TO THE WORK OF THE LORD, BECAUSE YOU KNOW THAT YOUR LABOR IN THE LORD IS NOT IN VAIN.

1 CORINTHIANS 15:58

DATE: _____

I HAVE SEEN THE HANDS OF GOD IN MY LIFE:

_____
_____
_____
_____
_____

TODAY'S SCRIPTURE READING

SCRIPTURE REFLECTIONS:

PRAYER LIST:

_____
_____
_____
_____
_____

DEAR GOD,

Consider it pure joy,
my brothers and sisters,
whenever you face trials of
many kinds, because you
know that the testing of your
faith produces perseverance.
Let perseverance finish its
work so that you may be
mature and complete, not
lacking anything.

JAMES 1:2-4

DATE: _____

I AM GRATEFUL FOR:

TODAY'S SCRIPTURE READING

_____

_____

SCRIPTURE REFLECTIONS:

_____

_____

_____

DEAR GOD,

I AM PRAYING FOR

PERSONAL   OTHERS

> I WILL INSTRUCT YOU AND TEACH YOU IN THE WAY YOU SHOULD GO; I WILL COUNSEL YOU WITH MY LOVING EYE ON YOU.
>
> **PSALM 32:8**

DATE: _____

I HAVE SEEN THE HANDS OF GOD IN MY LIFE:

_____
_____
_____
_____
_____
_____

TODAY'S SCRIPTURE READING

SCRIPTURE REFLECTIONS:

DOODLE HOW YOU REALLY FEEL TODAY

AREAS YOU WANT TO WORK ON:

_____
_____
_____
_____

1 PETER 2:24

He himself bore our sins in his body on the cross, so that we might die to sins and live for righteousness; By his wounds you have been Healed.

DATE: _____

TODAY I AM GRATEFUL FOR:

_____
_____
_____
_____
_____
_____

TODAY'S SCRIPTURE READING

SCRIPTURE REFLECTIONS:

DEAR GOD,

I AM PRAYING FOR:

_____
_____
_____
_____
_____

THE LORD MAKES FIRM THE STEPS OF THE ONE WHO DELIGHTS IN HIM; THOUGH HE MAY STUMBLE, HE WILL NOT FALL, FOR THE LORD UPHOLDS HIM WITH HIS HAND.

PSALM 37:23-24

DATE: _____

I HAVE SEEN THE HANDS OF GOD IN MY LIFE:

_____
_____
_____
_____
_____
_____

TODAY'S SCRIPTURE READING

SCRIPTURE REFLECTIONS:

PRAYER LIST:

_____
_____
_____
_____
_____

DEAR GOD,

The LORD will fight for you; you need only to be still.

EXODUS 14:14

DATE: _____

I AM GRATEFUL FOR: TODAY'S SCRIPTURE READING

_____

_____   SCRIPTURE REFLECTIONS:

_____

_____

_____

_____

DEAR GOD,

                    I AM PRAYING FOR
        PERSONAL   OTHERS

And we know that in all things God works for the good of those who love him, who have been called according to his purpose.

ROMANS 8:28

DATE: _____

I HAVE SEEN THE HANDS OF GOD IN MY LIFE:

_____
_____
_____
_____
_____
_____

TODAY'S SCRIPTURE READING

SCRIPTURE REFLECTIONS:

DOODLE HOW YOU REALLY FEEL TODAY

AREAS YOU WANT TO WORK ON:

_____
_____
_____
_____

ISAIAH 41:13

For I am the LORD your God who takes hold of your right hand and says to you, Do not fear; I will help you.

DATE: _____

TODAY I AM GRATEFUL FOR:

TODAY'S SCRIPTURE READING

SCRIPTURE REFLECTIONS:

DEAR GOD,

I AM PRAYING FOR:

IF ANY OF YOU LACKS WISDOM, YOU SHOULD ASK GOD, WHO GIVES GENEROUSLY TO ALL WITHOUT FINDING FAULT, AND IT WILL BE GIVEN TO YOU.

JAMES 1:5

DATE: _____

I HAVE SEEN THE HANDS OF GOD IN MY LIFE:

_____
_____
_____
_____
_____
_____

TODAY'S SCRIPTURE READING

SCRIPTURE REFLECTIONS:

PRAYER LIST:

_____
_____
_____
_____
_____

DEAR GOD,

If my people, who are called by my name, will humble themselves and pray and seek my face and turn from their wicked ways, then I will hear from heaven, and I will forgive their sin and will heal their land.

2 CHRONICLES 7:14

DATE: _____

I AM GRATEFUL FOR:

TODAY'S SCRIPTURE READING

_____

_____

SCRIPTURE REFLECTIONS:

_____

_____

_____

_____

DEAR GOD,

I AM PRAYING FOR

PERSONAL　　　　　　　OTHERS

EVEN THOUGH I WALK
THROUGH THE
DARKEST VALLEY,
I WILL FEAR NO EVIL,
FOR YOU ARE WITH
ME; YOUR ROD AND
YOUR STAFF,
THEY COMFORT ME.

JEREMIAH 29:12

DATE: _____

I HAVE SEEN THE HANDS OF GOD IN MY LIFE:

_____
_____
_____
_____
_____
_____

TODAY'S SCRIPTURE READING

SCRIPTURE REFLECTIONS:

DOODLE HOW YOU REALLY FEEL TODAY

AREAS YOU WANT TO WORK ON:

_____
_____
_____
_____

PROVERBS 3:5-6

Trust in the LORD with all your heart and lean not on your own understanding; in all your ways submit to him, and he will make your paths straight.

DATE: _____

TODAY I AM GRATEFUL FOR:

TODAY'S SCRIPTURE READING

SCRIPTURE REFLECTIONS:

DEAR GOD,

I AM PRAYING FOR:

SO I SAY TO YOU:
ASK AND IT WILL BE GIVEN
TO YOU;
SEEK AND YOU WILL FIND;
KNOCK AND THE DOOR WILL BE
OPENED TO YOU.
FOR EVERYONE WHO ASKS
RECEIVES;
THE ONE WHO SEEKS FINDS;
AND TO THE ONE WHO KNOCKS,
THE DOOR WILL BE OPENED.

LUKE 11:9-10

DATE: _____

I HAVE SEEN THE HANDS OF GOD IN MY LIFE:

_____
_____
_____
_____
_____
_____

TODAY'S SCRIPTURE READING

SCRIPTURE REFLECTIONS:

PRAYER LIST:

_____
_____
_____
_____
_____

DEAR GOD,

Who shall separate us
from the love of Christ?
Shall trouble or hardship
or persecution or famine or
nakedness or danger
or sword?

ROMANS 8:35

DATE: _____

I AM GRATEFUL FOR:

TODAY'S SCRIPTURE READING

_____

_____

SCRIPTURE REFLECTIONS:

_____

_____

_____

_____

DEAR GOD,

I AM PRAYING FOR

PERSONAL   OTHERS

> FOR THE SPIRIT GOD GAVE US DOES NOT MAKE US TIMID, BUT GIVES US POWER, LOVE AND SELF-DISCIPLINE.
>
> 2 TIMOTHY 1:7

DATE: _____

I HAVE SEEN THE HANDS OF GOD IN MY LIFE:

_____
_____
_____
_____
_____
_____

TODAY'S SCRIPTURE READING

SCRIPTURE REFLECTIONS:

DOODLE HOW YOU REALLY FEEL TODAY

AREAS YOU WANT TO WORK ON:

_____
_____
_____
_____

PSALM 144:1

*Praise the Lord,
my Rock,
who trains me for war,
who trains me for battle.*

DATE: _____

TODAY I AM GRATEFUL FOR:

_____
_____
_____
_____
_____
_____

TODAY'S SCRIPTURE READING

SCRIPTURE REFLECTIONS:

DEAR GOD,

I AM PRAYING FOR:

_____
_____
_____
_____
_____

"CALL TO ME AND I WILL ANSWER YOU AND TELL YOU GREAT AND UNSEARCHABLE THINGS YOU DO NOT KNOW."

JEREMIAH 33:3

DATE: _____

I HAVE SEEN THE HANDS OF GOD IN MY LIFE:

_____
_____
_____
_____
_____
_____

TODAY'S SCRIPTURE READING

SCRIPTURE REFLECTIONS:

PRAYER LIST:

_____
_____
_____
_____
_____

DEAR GOD,

Therefore put on the full armor of God, so that when the day of evil comes, you may be able to stand your ground, and after you have done everything, to stand.

EPHESIANS 6:13

DATE: _____

I AM GRATEFUL FOR:	TODAY'S SCRIPTURE READING

_____

_____	SCRIPTURE REFLECTIONS:

_____

_____

_____

_____

DEAR GOD,

I AM PRAYING FOR
PERSONAL			OTHERS

> WHEN YOU PRAY,
> GO INTO YOUR ROOM,
> CLOSE THE DOOR AND
> PRAY TO YOUR FATHER,
> WHO IS UNSEEN.
> THEN YOUR FATHER,
> WHO SEES WHAT IS
> DONE IN SECRET,
> WILL REWARD YOU.
>
> MATTHEW 6:6

DATE: _____

I HAVE SEEN THE HANDS OF GOD IN MY LIFE:

_____
_____
_____
_____
_____
_____

TODAY'S SCRIPTURE READING

SCRIPTURE REFLECTIONS:

DOODLE HOW YOU REALLY FEEL TODAY

AREAS YOU WANT TO WORK ON:

_____
_____
_____
_____

1 TIMOTHY 6:12

Fight the good fight of the faith. Take hold of the eternal life to which you were called when you made your good confession in the presence of many witnesses.

DATE: _____

TODAY I AM GRATEFUL FOR:

TODAY'S SCRIPTURE READING

_____

_____

SCRIPTURE REFLECTIONS:

_____

_____

_____

_____

DEAR GOD,

I AM PRAYING FOR:

_____

_____

_____

_____

_____

CONTINUE PRAYING, KEEPING ALERT, AND ALWAYS THANKING GOD.

COLOSSIANS 4:2

DATE: _____

I HAVE SEEN THE HANDS OF GOD IN MY LIFE:

_____
_____
_____
_____
_____

TODAY'S SCRIPTURE READING

SCRIPTURE REFLECTIONS:

PRAYER LIST:

_____
_____
_____
_____
_____

DEAR GOD,

The Lord will march out
like a strong soldier;
he will be excited like a
man ready to fight a war.
He will shout out the
battle cry and defeat
his enemies.

ISAIAH 42:13

DATE: _____

I AM GRATEFUL FOR:

TODAY'S SCRIPTURE READING

_____

_____

SCRIPTURE REFLECTIONS:

_____

_____

_____

_____

DEAR GOD,

I AM PRAYING FOR

PERSONAL   OTHERS

CERTIFICATE

OF COMMITMENT

FOR

PRAYER WARRIOR

Proudly presented to

_____

"THE EFFECTIVE PRAYER OF A RIGHTEOUS PERSON ACCOMPLISHES MUCH."

JAMES 5:16

Printed in Great Britain
by Amazon